LEGACY
of LESSONS

Interior photographs and letters are from the author's family collection and used with permission.

Nancy Moorhouse
Choteau, MT

Limits of Liability
The author and publisher shall not be liable for your misuse of this material. This book is strictly for informational and educational purposes.

Disclaimer
This book educates and entertains. The author and/or publisher guarantee no one following these techniques, suggestions, tips, ideas, or strategies will become successful. The author and/or publisher shall have neither liability nor responsibility to anyone regarding any loss or damage caused, or alleged to be caused, directly or indirectly by the information in this book.

Paperback ISBN: 979-8-9925484-5-7
eBook ISBN: 979-8-9925484-4-0

LEGACY
of LESSONS

How Family Can Reveal Learned Lessons And True Legacy

NANCY MOORHOUSE

THE LEGACY OF LESSONS FAMILIES LEAVE BEHIND

An old gray shoebox surrounded by a large Kmart plastic bag held the black and white photograph album on the top shelf in Grandma's hall closet. Visiting Grandma as a kid, she asked if I was interested in a little history.

Her recliner made a soft squeak as she gently rocked back and forth, and I laid the closet treasure in her lap. I drew up a kitchen chair as we settled in her front room; a picture of my dad was prominent on the top of the television console.

Grandma gently patted the shoebox and slowly removed its top. Inside were tightly tucked blue envelopes, each handwritten to her and Grandpa. She showed me one and I admired the two-cent postage stamp, the cancelled postage mark, and recognized my dad's handwriting. She carefully removed the letter inside. It was a letter dad had written to her and Grandpa when he was 18 years old and stationed in the Marshall Islands from 1944 and 1945. She set the letter and envelope on her chest as I handed her the album. She delicately opened the album cover where she had saved the pictures he sent home as an enlistee.

Grandma kept each of his letters, a memory of her son who had quit high school to enlist in the US Navy. Each of the treasured letters had personal accounts of boot camp, life on an atoll, the USS Lexington and requests to get his high school diploma while stationed over 6,500 miles from home.

Grandma is gone; dad has passed. He would not speak of his war years while I was growing up. His only request of me was to visit the Pearl Harbor memorial for those who lost their lives on December 7, 1941.

Questions I now have remain unanswered. But I have understandings through his World War 2 correspondence written home. Eighty-year-old letters bringing insights of my dad as a young man who experienced war, returning home to find peace, purpose, love. Oh, how these letters are a gift of legacy and a young life well done.

ENTRIES

PATIENCE

Waking up, going through the familiar morning rituals, facing the long hours of a work day, coming home exhausted, and tending to the usual evening tasks—all carried out in a quiet, rhythmic way, almost without thinking. These actions form the backbone of Grandma's days. A daily routine, repeated so often that it feels like the worn tracks left behind by passing vehicles in the dirt. There is a comfort in that repetition, a soft lull that settles over the soul like a familiar blanket.

And then, a sudden, dramatic shift. Her only son enlists in the military and is sent over 7,000 miles to serve his country in the Marshall Islands. The war is far from home, across the ocean, and their only connection now is through telegrams and handwritten letters taking weeks to arrive. In the silence between messages, she fills her time with more busyness—taking on extra chores, lingering over errands—trying to stay occupied. But even the smallest disruptions seem louder, sharper. Little distractions that once passed unnoticed now irritate her like tiny grains of sand in a shoe.

"Remain calm," she tells herself repeatedly. "The mailman will bring a letter from my son today."

And one day, he does. The envelope, worn and creased from its long journey, is handed to her with a simple nod. She holds it in trembling hands, breathes in deeply, and carefully opens it. Her son's words, scrawled in his familiar handwriting, reach across the distance and settle her heart. She reads and rereads every line, each sentence like a balm to her soul.

With every letter that arrives, she finds herself able to breathe a little easier. Each brings a touch more strength.

More courage. And most of all, more patience with the long, uncertain days of war in the Pacific.

The steady comfort of a letter from the son she loves so deeply—each one a quiet lesson in enduring love. Teaching her to face hardship not with fear, but with hope. To meet long waiting not with frustration, but with grace. To hold on, even when it hurts. To grow in the quiet power of patience.

The Value of Patience

Patience is often mistaken for passivity, for simply waiting without protest. Yet, the patience that carries us through life's most difficult seasons is not weak or silent. It is active, intentional, and rooted in strength. My grandmother's waiting was not idle; it was a discipline. Every day she chose to trust that a letter would come, even when the silence stretched. That choice shaped her, giving her courage when her heart could have been consumed by fear.

When we think about patience, we often picture a pause—a waiting room, a stalled moment in time. But true patience is not about stopping. It is about continuing, even while uncertain. It is showing up to the day with steadiness when the outcome has yet to be revealed. It is the practice of living in the "not yet," of inhabiting the in-between without losing hope.

In a world that prizes speed, patience can feel like an inconvenience, even a weakness. Our culture rewards quick solutions, instant gratification, and rapid responses.

But what happens when life refuses to cooperate with those timelines? Illness does not resolve overnight. Dreams do not blossom immediately. Broken relationships do not mend in an instant. In those seasons, patience becomes a virtue and a survival skill.

Patience allows us to soften our grip on control. It reminds us that much of life cannot be forced. Like seeds in the ground, some things require time, warmth, and care to grow. No amount of tugging at the stalk will hasten the harvest. Patience teaches us to nurture rather than demand, to tend rather than rush, and to believe that time itself has wisdom we cannot match.

There is also a deep humility in patience. It acknowledges that we are not the masters of every outcome. My father, stationed thousands of miles away, could not hurry the mail ship that carried his letters. My grandmother could not change where he was stationed or shorten his service. But she could control how she responded. She could practice patience in the face of uncertainty, filling her days with small acts of love, holding fast to her faith, and waiting with grace. That patience did not change the war, but it changed her.

The gift of patience is how it reshapes our inner life. Without it, worry and frustration take root, gnawing at our peace. With it, we find ourselves breathing easier, even in struggle. Patience steadies the heart. It lengthens our perspective, helping us to see beyond the urgency of today into the wider picture of tomorrow. When practiced well, it helps us listen more deeply, love more generously, and live with a gentler spirit.

In practical ways, patience can transform relationships.

Consider the difference between reacting in irritation and pausing to listen. A single breath, a moment of restraint, can prevent an argument from taking root. In friendships, marriages, and family ties, patience is the soil where trust and understanding can grow. Without it, harsh words are spoken too quickly, decisions are made without thought, and bonds can fray. With it, space is given for others to be imperfect, for reconciliation to happen, for love to last.

Patience also strengthens resilience. Life will test us with disappointments, setbacks, and unanswered prayers. If we rush to abandon hope at the first sign of difficulty, we rob ourselves of growth. But patience keeps us in the process. It allows us to persevere long enough to see results we might have missed had we given up too soon. Think of the craftsman refining his skill, the gardener waiting for blossoms, the student persisting through years of study— each is practicing patience, and each will eventually reap the fruit of their persistence.

Even in small, daily ways, patience offers peace. Waiting in traffic, standing in line, navigating delays—these moments become lighter when met with acceptance rather than anger. Each is an invitation to release tension, to practice presence, to notice life unfolding around us. Caught in waiting, we may discover something unexpected: a moment of stillness we would otherwise have missed.

Ultimately, patience is an act of love. It is love for ourselves, giving grace when we falter. It is love for others, allowing them to grow and stumble without condemnation. And it is love for life itself, trusting that what is meant to come will arrive in its time.

When my grandmother held my father's letters, she

was not only practicing patience with the war and the distance—she was practicing love. Love that waited. Love that endured silence. Love that held on until the words on thin paper found their way across the ocean. In her waiting, she modeled the truth that patience is not merely a delay; it is devotion stretched across time.

Reflection Questions

Where in my life am I resisting patience?
Consider a place where you are pushing for quick results, whether in relationships, work, or personal growth. How might patience shift your perspective or open a gentler path forward?

What practices can help me wait with grace?
Identify small habits—deep breathing, journaling, prayer, mindful walks—that can transform moments of waiting into opportunities for growth.

How can I view waiting as active rather than passive?
Instead of seeing patience as "doing nothing," explore what supportive actions you can take while waiting— nurturing relationships, tending to self-care, or preparing for the next step.

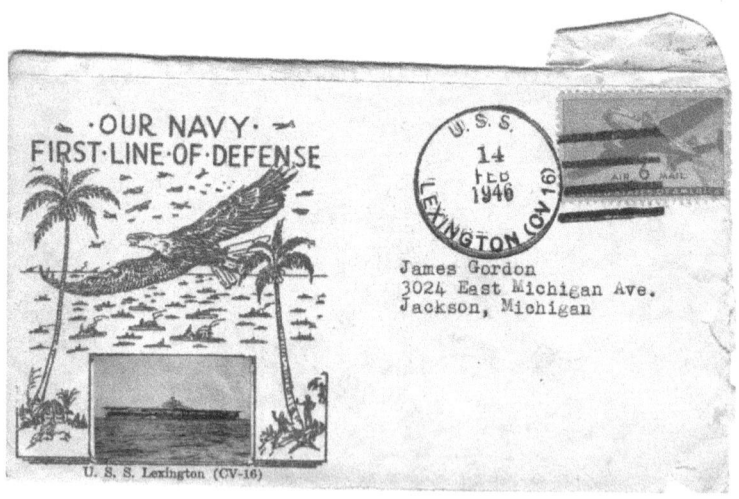

- ·OUR NAVY· -
FIRST·LINE·OF·DEFENSE

U. S. S.
14
FEB
1946
LEXINGTON (CV 16)

AIR MAIL

James Gordon
3024 East Michigan Ave.
Jackson, Michigan

U. S. S. Lexington (CV-16)

ENDURANCE

Fundamentals must be mastered before moving on to the next challenge. For young Navy men in boot camp, the grinder referred to a wide, unforgiving concrete area used for relentless physical training and the endless repetitions of close-order drill instruction. Marching was more than routine—it was life itself. Drill sergeants seemed merciless, pushing recruits through mile after mile, hour after hour of marching, until their legs ached and their minds surrendered. The drill was designed to give the recruits something that at first felt impossible, to force them to work and sweat and stumble until they discovered they could do it, and then to start all over again the next day.

Trust and fear were the forces that drove the grinder. The routine was drilled into them day after day, repeatedly, grinding each recruit's soul into shape, pushing them toward discipline and unity. Tomorrow's drill was always meant to be better than today's. They had to show up ready, no matter how blistered their feet or how raw their voices from calling cadence. Each day, each hour, they learned endurance. They learned to keep going even when they wanted to stop.

Some days in my own life feel like those old grinder days my dad wrote about. When the weedwhacker refuses to start, the wind keeps slapping dust in my face, when the dog ignoring his name being called, charges off into the empty wheat field after a rabbit. On those days, I remind myself, "It's a grinder kind of day." And I keep going. I stick with it, even when every part of me wants to quit, even when nothing seems to work. Because showing up matters. Endurance matters. It is not about winning or finishing quickly—it is about staying in the fight, trusting the process, and proving to yourself that you will not back down.

A grinder day teaches me the same lesson those young recruits learned on the concrete: to keep showing up. To put one foot in front of the other. To endure. To trust the process.

The Value of Endurance

Endurance is more than the ability to push through pain or hardship. It is the art of holding steady when everything inside you whispers it would be easier to stop. On the grinder at boot camp, my father and the other young recruits learned this lesson step by step, march by march. Their muscles ached, their voices cracked from cadence, and still they pressed on. What looked like merciless repetition was training for life. They were being shaped into men who would not quit when circumstances grew hard.

Endurance is the quiet partner of hope. Hope gives us the vision of what could be. Endurance provides the strength to keep walking toward it, even when obstacles rise in the way. Without endurance, hope falters. Without hope, endurance has no direction. Together, they form the backbone of perseverance.

We often imagine endurance as belonging only to the battlefield, the athletic field, or the arena of grand challenges. But most of us meet endurance in far smaller, more ordinary ways. It is the parent waking through the night with a restless child. It is the worker showing up day after day, even when the tasks feel endless. It is the caregiver who keeps loving and tending when gratitude is scarce and fatigue is heavy. In each of these places, endurance is not glamorous. It is not applauded. Yet it is holy in its persistence, because it transforms both the one who endures and those who are touched by their perseverance.

There is a rhythm to endurance. It is rarely about sudden bursts of energy or heroic effort. More often, it is the steady placing of one foot after another, the commitment to get through today without giving up. That rhythm builds strength. Just as muscles are formed by repeated strain and release, our character grows through consistent, often unseen acts of endurance.

Endurance also teaches humility. We learn quickly that willpower alone cannot carry us forever. Fatigue comes. Doubt whispers. The body and spirit reach their limits. In those moments, endurance shifts from self-reliance to trust. Trust in the process, trust in others, trust in something greater than ourselves. My father's letters from boot camp carried that spirit. He did not simply describe the grind. He revealed what it taught him: that tomorrow could be better than today, that unity with others mattered, that showing up despite pain was the truest measure of strength.

When we practice endurance in our own lives, we become people of stability. Others know they can rely on us. We learn that commitment matters more than comfort. Our children, our friends, our coworkers see in us a model of perseverance, and in turn they find courage for their own paths. Endurance ripples outward, giving strength to those who watch us keep going.

There is also a hidden gift in endurance: perspective. When you endure hardship, what once seemed impossible becomes manageable. The mountain shrinks, not because it is smaller but because you have grown stronger. Looking back, you see that the pain which once felt overwhelming was forming resilience. That realization becomes fuel for the future. You begin to trust that if you could withstand the storm of yesterday, you can face the challenges of tomorrow.

Endurance shapes how we approach time. In a culture addicted to shortcuts, endurance calls us to slow down and remain steady. It whispers that great things take time, that the best fruits often come after long cultivation. The runner finishes the marathon not because of one day's effort, but because of months of practice. The student earns a degree not in a single evening but after years of steady study. The garden blooms only after seasons of tending. Endurance is the thread that ties all worthwhile achievements together.

And yet endurance is not simply gritting your teeth and suffering. It is about choosing meaning in the struggle. My father's grinder days were miserable at times, but they were not pointless. Each mile marched was shaping discipline, preparing for real battles that lay ahead. In the same way, our trials may feel senseless in the moment, but endurance invites us to search for purpose. What is this hardship teaching me? Who am I becoming through this? Those questions turn endurance from mere survival into transformation.

There is also joy hidden within endurance. Not the immediate joy of ease, but the deep joy of looking back and knowing you did not quit. Few feelings compare to the satisfaction of finishing something that once seemed unbearable. That joy is sweeter precisely because it was hard won. Endurance makes that joy possible, for it carries us across the long distance between beginning and completion.

In life, everyone faces "grinder days." The times when nothing seems to work, when progress feels invisible, when exhaustion presses hard. On those days, endurance calls us to remember: showing up matters. Effort matters. Trusting the process matters. Endurance may not make life easier, but it makes us stronger, steadier, and more faithful to the path laid before us.

Reflection Questions

Where in my life do I need endurance more than instant results?
Reflect on areas where you want quick fixes or fast success. How might enduring the slow process lead to deeper growth or more lasting change?

What practices help me keep going when I feel like quitting?
Identify small anchors—daily routines, supportive relationships, words of encouragement—that help you endure difficult days.

How can I see meaning in the hardships I face?
Consider what lessons, strengths, or new perspectives might be forming in you through your current challenges.

UNITED STATES NAVAL TRAINING STATION
FARRAGUT, IDAHO

LEGACY

When I had the chance to visit with Grandma Gordon, she would often drift back into memories of my dad's younger days. I only knew him as the older man who married my mom and raised three spirited daughters.

Somehow, I never pictured my dad as a young man. He was always just Dad, steady and practical, someone I relied on. Now, decades later, I wonder about his life before us. He died a month after I turned eighteen. I was too young to truly reflect on his journey or think much about what he left behind. But time changes how you see things. Now he is gone, his voice a memory, and I want to understand the man he was before he became my father.

One treasure remains: a shoebox of his World War II Navy letters. Grandma saved them carefully. These fragile pieces of paper, dated from 1944 to 1946, offer a window into a world I never knew. They reveal a young man growing from adolescent into adult, facing war and uncertainty, sending words of hope and love to his mother back home. Each letter feels like a gift, a bridge between past and present. As I read them, I find tears in my eyes and a quiet joy in my heart. I see his fascination with mechanics, his appreciation for beauty, and the value he placed on education and learning.

This small box of letters is much more than paper and ink. It is a legacy, a gift of love from son to mother, now resting in my hands. It reminds me that the stories of our lives matter and that what we do and say continues long after we are gone. Family history keeps those memories alive. These letters let my dad's spirit and voice live on, his love reaching across time, showing me he left something lasting behind. Written letters became a gift to his mother, and now they are a gift. A reminder of his legacy, and how love endures.

The Value of Legacy

Legacy is often misunderstood as something grand; something left only by leaders, inventors, or public figures whose names are carved into history. Yet legacy lives in much quieter places. It is found in the way a father's handwritten letters cross the decades, carrying his voice into the hands of his grown child. In the shoebox, sat tucked in a closet, holding memories that waited patiently to be rediscovered. Legacy is not only what we accomplish, but also what we preserve, what we pass on, and what we choose to live by.

When I think of legacy, I think of time stretching in both directions. Behind us are the people who shaped us—parents, grandparents, teachers, mentors—who left impressions on our lives whether they realized it. Ahead of us are those who will remember us: children, friends, coworkers, neighbors. What connects both directions are the way we choose to live today. Legacy is not built only after death; it is written daily in how we speak, how we act, and how we love.

The letters my father sent home are a powerful example of this truth. As a young man far from home, he was not writing with legacy in mind. He was sharing his thoughts, describing his days, sending comfort across an ocean. Yet those words became more than ink on paper. They became a bridge. They allowed his mother to know her son in real time, and they allow me, decades later, to know him as a young man. What he could not have imagined then is that his letters would live on as his legacy, a reminder of who he was and what he valued.

Legacy is less about wealth or possessions than it is about values and presence. A man or woman may leave behind no money, but if they leave behind kindness, wisdom, or courage, then their legacy is rich. The best legacies are not measured in bank accounts or property deeds. They are measured in the love we give, the faith we hold, the character we model. These endure beyond the moment and take root in others' lives.

Legacy also carries responsibility. Once we recognize that what we do today echoes tomorrow, our choices take on weight. Do we live in a way we want to be remembered? Do we speak words we would want written down? Each moment offers an opportunity to shape the legacy we leave. That awareness can sober us, but it can also inspire us. We realize that even small acts of generosity or encouragement are not wasted. They may outlast us in ways we cannot predict.

At its heart, legacy is about connection. It ties generations together, reminding us that our lives are not isolated but part of a larger story. My father's letters do not belong only to me. They carry pieces of him that belong to his mother, his family, and now to anyone who reads them. In the same way, each of us has something to pass along. It may be a story, a lesson, a piece of wisdom, or the way we lived faithfully in ordinary days.

One of the greatest gifts of legacy is perspective. It pulls us out of the narrow view of today's problems and reminds us that our lives have longer arcs. Hardships that feel overwhelming may look different when we think about what kind of story we want to tell years from now. Legacy invites us to ask: How do I want to be remembered? What values do I want to live so consistently that others associate them with me? These questions change how we approach even small decisions, because we see them as threads in a much larger tapestry.

Legacy is also about healing. Sometimes what we inherit from the past is brokenness—habits of neglect, cycles of harm, silence where there should have been love. Here, too, we can shape a new legacy. Choosing forgiveness, choosing to live differently, choosing to break patterns of harm—these are ways of building legacies of restoration. We may not control what was handed to us, but we can influence what we hand forward.

And legacy is not only about family bloodlines. Each of us touches circles wider than our kin. We shape the communities where we live, the workplaces we enter, the friendships we form. Our words, actions, and presence ripple outward. A kind teacher's encouragement may guide a student's career. A neighbor's steady kindness may change how a child views the world. In these ways, our legacies multiply far beyond what we see.

The shoebox of letters taught me this: what seems ordinary in the moment may become extraordinary later. A letter written in haste becomes a treasure decades on. A story told in passing becomes an anchor of memory. A decision to live with integrity becomes a model for the next generation. This is why legacy matters: because our days are not wasted, and our choices do not vanish. They linger, shaping the lives that follow.

To live with legacy in mind is not to become consumed with how others will think of us. It is to live fully awake to the meaning of our actions. It is to remember that love and truth echo longer than we can measure. It is to understand that while none of us is perfect, we all have something worth passing on.

Reflection Questions

What values do I want to be remembered for?
Consider the traits or principles that matter most to you.
Are you living in a way that makes them visible to others?

What am I passing on, intentionally or unintentionally?
Think about your daily habits, words, and attitudes. What
legacy are they building even in small ways?

How can I preserve and share the legacies given to me?
Reflect on the lessons, stories, or examples from those
who came before you. How can you honor and carry them
forward for others?

FOCUS

One of my favorite letters my dad wrote home on September 14, 1944:

This morning at 6:30 the Captain gave the order for everyone to turn to and help clean up the Island (or else no beer). Well, my job was to clean up around our office and there was quite a bit of junk under the office. It sets up on one foot block, so I asked my Commanding Officer if it would be O.K. for me to get a truck and make a little rock garden around the office and he said for me to go ahead.

And while I was driving among some trees, (I had a ten-wheel truck), I drove over a stump and then I decided to back up into a nice spot where the rock pile was. Well, while I was backing up, all of a sudden my truck stopped and it wouldn't go ahead or back up. So, I got out to see what the trouble was and both (8 duals) back duals were off of the ground, so I kicked the front wheel drive in and that didn't help so I released the winch, and hooked it to a tree then kicked it into gear and it pulled the truck off of the stump and the knot in the cable tightened up so that we couldn't get it off the tree. So, I get a hacksaw and cut it off and I had my load of rocks.

Reading this letter repeatedly, I am struck by the clear-headed focus he had in what could have been a frustrating and confusing mess. He took a situation that might have rattled others and instead found a way forward, calmly using what was available, thinking through the next step, and moving on with determination. He did not complain about the stump or curse the cable or abandon the task. He focused on the goal: gathering rocks to make a small garden around the office, doing his part to improve the place.

His words spill out in a matter-of-fact way, filled with practical details that reveal not just skill but a quiet confidence and a deep focus on finishing what he started. Even when the truck was stuck, even when the winch cable refused to budge, he kept his mind steady on the job. That focus is what turns small chores into accomplishments, what makes a simple load of rocks into something meaningful.

In every line, I hear the pride of someone who knows the power of staying locked in, of paying attention, of using every tool and option before him. The story shows me how focus can carry us through unexpected challenges and turn a minor disaster into a small victory, reminding me again why this letter means so much.

The Value of Focus

Focus is the ability to hold steady when distractions or frustrations pull at us. It is the discipline of giving our full attention to what matters most in the moment, resisting the urge to scatter our energy in too many directions. My father's story of the stuck truck on the island could easily have turned into chaos or defeat. Instead, he chose clarity. He assessed the problem, tried different solutions, and kept his mind on the task until he found a way forward. That simple load of rocks became a small monument to the power of focus.

Focus is rarely about grand concentration in perfect conditions. More often it is forged in imperfection—when noise, pressure, and setbacks tempt us to quit or lash out.

To remain focused in those moments requires self-control, perspective, and a willingness to choose calm over chaos. It requires us to resist the scattered energy of frustration and instead channel our efforts toward the next step forward.

In daily life, focus is constantly tested. We live in a world filled with distractions. Our phones buzz, notifications clamor, and countless voices compete for our attention. The ability to focus has never been more valuable, because it allows us to reclaim the power of intentional living. Without focus, our days slip away in fragments, each interruption pulling us further from what matters. With focus, we make deliberate progress toward our goals, our relationships, and the kind of lives we want to live.

Focus also helps us in moments of difficulty. Problems often feel larger when we view them as a tangled mass of obstacles. Focus breaks them down into smaller pieces. What is the real issue? What is the next action? Like my father dealing with the truck and cable, clarity emerges when we focus on the step directly in front of us rather than the entire weight of the problem. This mindset keeps panic at bay and allows solutions to appear.

There is also a moral dimension to focus. What we focus on shapes who we become. If we give our constant attention to negativity, gossip, or fear, those things grow stronger in our lives. If we choose instead to focus on gratitude, purpose, and love, then those qualities deepen. Focus acts as a lens, magnifying what we direct it toward. This is why cultivating intentional focus is so vital: it determines the direction of our growth.

Focus is not rigid. It does not mean we block out everything else or live with tunnel vision. Rather, it is about priority. It is the skill of deciding what deserves attention now and what can wait. It is knowing when to turn off the noise and give presence to a person in front of us. It is choosing to finish a task rather than jumping endlessly between half-started projects. In this way, focus brings order to our lives. It simplifies what feels overwhelming by reminding us: do one thing, and then the next.

There is freedom in focus. Many people believe focus is confining, as if paying attention to one thing means missing out on others. Yet, focus liberates us. It quiets the constant pull of distraction and allows us to experience life more deeply. A focused conversation is richer than a distracted one. A focused moment of prayer or meditation is more nourishing than scattered thoughts. A focused effort at work or in a hobby brings more satisfaction than multitasking. When we focus, we discover presence—and presence is where meaning lives.

Focus also builds confidence. Each time we give full attention to a task and see it through, we prove to ourselves that we are capable. The sense of completion, even in small things, accumulates. Over time, that confidence extends into larger challenges. The person who learns to focus on daily responsibilities is better prepared to stay steady in moments of crisis. This was true for my father. The ability to focus on a stuck truck was the same discipline that helped him endure the far greater tests of war.

In relationships, focus is a gift. Giving another person your full attention communicates value and respect. To listen deeply, without drifting or rushing, creates connection. Many conflicts can be softened or resolved simply by truly focusing on what someone else is saying. In an age where attention is fragmented, focused presence becomes an act of love.

Focus is also essential for legacy. The shoebox of letters would not exist had my father not taken time to focus on writing them. The lessons of patience and endurance would not be passed on if his mother had not focused on preserving them. What we focus on today often becomes the legacy others inherit.

Ultimately, focus is about alignment. It asks: Am I paying attention to what matters most? Am I pouring my energy into the things that last, or scattering it among the temporary and trivial? To cultivate focus is to live with intention, to give our best efforts not to everything but to the right things.

Reflection Questions

What distractions most often pull me away from what matters?
Identify the habits, technologies, or thoughts that scatter your attention. How can you limit or redirect them?

How can I break problems into smaller steps?
Consider an area of frustration in your life. What is one focused action you can take today to move forward, even if the full solution feels far away?

Who in my life needs more of my focused attention?
Reflect on relationships where you might be present physically but not fully engaged. What would it look like to focus on them more deeply?

"Majuro atoll"
ONE FLAG

ONE COUNTRY
12 January 1945

ALLEGIANCE

Dad, a gas pump jockey, started working at Leo's filling station at the start of his freshman year of high school. Dad learned mechanical skills on the old Model A he drove back and forth to the gas station taking special pride in the family's '38 Ford. Leo's filling station was not fancy, but it kept the community rolling, supplying gas, tires, and the occasional oil change. Leo treated Dad fairly, giving him steady work and even writing a letter of recommendation when Dad enlisted in the Navy.

When Dad wrote home during the war, he would always ask about the cars back home, wanting to know if they were simonized and running well, and if Leo was rationing gas like everyone else. But he also heard the gossip, the stories that Leo was still drinking too much, and how he had left his wife for another woman. That news did not sit well with Dad. Loyalty to family meant everything to him. He could not accept someone turning their back on vows or walking away from responsibility.

At twenty years old, stationed in the Marshall Islands far from home, he wrote to his parents:

"How is old drunken Leo coming? I hope that you aren't buying your gas there, and if he asks you why not, tell him I said so. Tell him I don't like guys that leave their wives."

Dad's allegiance to family, to integrity, to the people who showed up and stayed true, never wavered. It was the foundation of who he was. If someone crossed the line into unethical or immoral choices, he would not look the other way, no matter how long he had known them. Friendship or past kindness did not matter if the other person proved unworthy by their actions.

Divorced Leo, just thirty-two years old, died alone from delirium tremens. For Dad, there were lines you did not cross, and promises you did not break. Morality and allegiance were not empty words but guiding principles for how to live, how to treat others, and how to measure the true character of a man.

The Value of Allegiance

Allegiance is a word that speaks to loyalty, devotion, and unwavering commitment. It is the steady anchor that holds us in place when the world pulls in different directions. My father's feelings toward Leo, the filling station owner who abandoned his family, reveal the seriousness with which he regarded allegiance. To him, loyalty was not negotiable. Promises mattered. Faithfulness to family was not an option, but a moral obligation. In his eyes, someone who broke that bond forfeited trust.

Allegiance begins with choosing where our loyalties lie. Every day, whether we recognize it or not, we pledge ourselves to certain people, causes, and values. Some allegiances are formal—marriage vows, national oaths, sworn duties. Others are quieter but no less powerful—commitments to loved ones, fidelity to personal values, loyalty to community. Together, these allegiances shape our character. They reveal what we hold most sacred and what kind of people we want to be remembered as.

In a culture where promises are often broken and commitments quickly abandoned, allegiance shines as a rare virtue. It calls us to stand firm, to stay true even when circumstances change, even when temptation whispers that it would be easier to walk away. Allegiance is not blind stubbornness, but clear-eyed devotion. It is knowing that loyalty to what is right requires sacrifice, yet choosing it anyway.

At its deepest level, allegiance reflects integrity. It is the outward expression of inner conviction. A person of allegiance does not change their principles when it becomes inconvenient. They remain faithful, not because it is easy, but because it is right. This is why my father could not ignore Leo's betrayal of his family. For him, allegiance was not just about showing up at work or fulfilling a duty. It was about living so your word and your life matched.

Allegiance also builds trust. Relationships thrive when people know they can depend on one another. A marriage grows when both partners honor their vows through good and bad seasons. Friendships deepen when loyalty proves stronger than distance or disagreement. Communities flourish when members stand with each other in times of need. Allegiance turns fleeting connections into lasting bonds, weaving stability into the fabric of human life.

Yet allegiance is not without cost. It asks us to place others before ourselves. It requires us to endure difficulties rather than abandoning commitments when they become burdensome. Allegiance sometimes means saying no to personal gain for the sake of staying faithful to a promise. These sacrifices can be difficult in the moment, but they shape us into people of substance, people whose lives reflect courage and devotion.

There is also a caution in allegiance. Misplaced loyalty

can bind us to unhealthy or destructive paths. Allegiance must be joined with wisdom. It is not about standing by wrongdoing or staying loyal to harmful behavior. True allegiance aligns itself with integrity, truth, and love. It calls us to discern what is worthy of our devotion and to stand firm in those places. My father understood this distinction. He could honor Leo as a man who once offered him work, but when Leo abandoned his wife, that bond of respect was broken. Allegiance, to him, was inseparable from morality.

In a broader sense, allegiance connects us to something greater than ourselves. It may be allegiance to faith, to a vision of justice, or to the enduring strength of family. Such allegiance provides direction in a world that often feels rootless. It reminds us that our lives are about personal comfort and about responsibility to others and to the values we profess.

Allegiance also shapes legacy. What we remain faithful to becomes part of what we leave behind. A life of loyalty teaches the next generation the worth of keeping promises. A life of consistency shows that stability and devotion matter more than temporary pleasures. My father's life, measured not by wealth but by integrity and commitment, continues to speak through the stories and letters preserved. His allegiance to family, to honesty, and to responsibility created a heritage far more enduring than any material possession could.

In our time, when distractions and shifting loyalties seem to rule, choosing allegiance can feel countercultural. But it is in that choice that we find strength and clarity. To commit ourselves deeply, to stand by our word, to honor our families, to align our loyalty with what is good—these are the actions that steady us and give meaning to our lives.

Reflection Questions

Where do my strongest allegiances lie?
Reflect on the people, values, or causes you are most devoted to. Are they the ones you want to shape your life and legacy?

How do I demonstrate loyalty in my daily life?
Consider the ways your actions reveal or undermine your commitments. Are you consistent in word and deed?

When should I reassess my allegiances?
Think about whether any loyalties in your life are misplaced or unhealthy. How can you realign your allegiance with integrity and love?

BLUE STAR
1ST WINDOW - AFTER
HE LEFT FOR
SERVICE march 1944 HIS BIKE
Sure LOOKSOME.

GUIDANCE

When you first arrived at boot camp, everything was new, fast, and a little overwhelming. You are in a sea of uniforms, barked orders, early mornings, and expectations. And then someone hands you a book with a deep navy-blue cover with gold lettering —*The Bluejackets' Manual,* by the United States Naval Institute. A firm, practical 585-page hardcover, roadmap to becoming a sailor, book.

It is the Navy's mentor in print form. In 1944, at 18 years old, my dad received his "bible" while at boot camp at Farragut Naval Training Station. To a young recruit, outside of his comfort zone, the manual felt like a rite of passage: "You're in the Navy now, sailor. Learn the ropes."

The Navy is full of history, pride, and structure, and the manual was his lifeline, his connection to all of it. It became his silent mentor and his go-to when alone in a bunk at night, wondering if he was cut out for this.

Outlining tasks to be learned, it helped him belong. The guidance was on page 3, stating the qualities of a good Navy man. A short list of ten qualities he wanted to emulate as a son, as a Navy man, and as an individual. Page 3 was dog-eared; one he would revisit to check his progress against each of the stated qualities.

Lifelines, teachers, traditions, mentors showing us, because yes, there is a right way. To a young recruit trying to find their footing in the U.S. Navy, page 3 was part lifeline, part teacher, and part tradition, all important things wrapped up on a single page. It was his north star.

The Value of Guidance

Guidance is the steady hand that shapes our path when we are unsure of the way forward. It may come in the form of a mentor, a trusted friend, a teacher, or even a book. For my father, it arrived in the form of *The Bluejackets' Manual*, pressed into his hands at Farragut Naval Training Station. That thick book of rules, lessons, and expectations was more than paper and ink. It was a compass. At eighteen years old, far from home and unsure of what awaited him, the manual became a source of stability and direction.

Guidance matters because no one enters life already knowing how to live it well. We are all beginners at the start of every stage—youth, adulthood, parenthood, leadership, aging. At each threshold, we need direction. Guidance provides it, not as a map that shows every detail, but as a set of principles, reminders, and practices that help us take the next right step. Without guidance, we wander. With it, we find footing.

The qualities on page three of that manual—qualities my father returned to often—were not simply naval instructions. They were life lessons: discipline, loyalty, courage, and integrity. These qualities gave him a standard to measure himself against and a vision for the man he wanted to become. Guidance provided clarity. In moments of confusion, it offered a reminder of what mattered. In moments of doubt, it gave him something to aspire toward.

In our own lives, guidance takes many forms. Sometimes it is explicit, like a book or a course of study. Other times it is subtle, like the example of a parent, the wisdom of a friend, or the quiet model of someone living with dignity.

To pay attention to such guidance is to recognize that wisdom is always near us if we will listen. The challenge is not the lack of guidance but our willingness to receive it.

Guidance also requires humility. To seek direction is to admit we do not know everything. That admission runs counter to pride, but it is the doorway to growth. The wisest people are those who remain teachable. They recognize that learning never ends and that guidance can arrive from unexpected places. Even a young sailor, sitting alone at night with a book, can find life-shaping wisdom in the printed page.

The absence of guidance can leave scars. Many who lack strong role models or steady mentors find themselves adrift, making avoidable mistakes and carrying unnecessary burdens. Yet the beauty of guidance is that it is never too late to seek. Books, communities, mentors, faith traditions—all offer direction at any stage of life. What matters is cultivating the openness to hear and the courage to follow.

Guidance also protects. It warns us against pitfalls and helps us avoid repeating the errors of others. Just as road signs mark dangerous curves, wise guidance cautions us where life's roads are risky. It may not shield us from every hardship, but it spares us unnecessary harm. It allows us to build on the lessons of others rather than learning everything by painful trial.

At the same time, guidance empowers. Good guidance does not create dependence; it fosters maturity. A mentor, teacher, or manual is not meant to control us but to equip us. It gives us tools and confidence to face the unknown.

My father may have leaned on *The Bluejackets' Manual* in his earliest days, but in time those principles became second nature. The guidance took root within him, forming part of his character, shaping how he lived long after the book was closed.

There is also a generational dimension to guidance. What we receive, we are called to pass on. My father learned qualities of discipline, integrity, and loyalty from his naval training, but he also modeled them at home. In that way, the guidance he received rippled outward into the next generation. We, too, carry this responsibility. The lessons we embrace today are not only for us—they are seeds planted for others who will walk behind us.

Guidance does not erase hardship. My father still faced danger, uncertainty, and loss. But it gave him a framework for facing them. In the same way, our own lives will always bring challenges. The question is not whether we will encounter them, but whether we will have guidance to carry us through. With guidance, storms can be faced with courage. Without it, storms can overwhelm us.

Ultimately, guidance is about orientation. It helps us keep our eyes on true north, reminding us of who we are and who we want to become. It calls us to accountability when we drift and gives encouragement when we falter. It is both anchor and light. Like my father turning back to page three of *The Bluejackets' Manual*, each of us needs something—or someone—that helps us measure where we stand and points us to where we should go.

Reflection Questions

Where am I seeking guidance?
Reflect on the sources you turn to when life feels uncertain.
Are they reliable, wise, and aligned with your values?

Am I teachable?
Consider whether pride or fear keeps you from receiving
guidance. How can you cultivate humility and openness
to learning?

What guidance am I passing on?
Think about the lessons you live out daily. How are your
actions serving as guidance for those who look to you?

EPILOGUE

A Legacy of Lessons

It began with a shoebox. A simple gray box, wrapped in a worn plastic bag, tucked away on a closet shelf. Inside, folded and saved with care, were letters from a young man to his mother and father. Those letters were not written with history in mind. They were daily reflections, stories of camp and duty, glimpses of frustration and pride. They were a son reaching across the miles to reassure, to share, to connect. He could not have known that decades later, those same words would teach lessons to his child, and perhaps to many others.

That is the hidden truth of legacy: it is not built only in grand gestures or historic moments. It is built quietly, day after day, in the choices we make and the values we live. My father's shoebox of letters is proof of this. What he lived—his patience, endurance, focus, allegiance, and openness to guidance—was written down in ordinary words, preserved by a mother's devotion, and handed forward into the hands of the next generation. Those lessons, once lived in the heat of war, became part of the family's inheritance.

Legacy is not only what we leave behind in objects or records. Legacy is the shaping of lives through example. Each letter, each decision, each small act of integrity, forms the soil from which others will learn. The lessons we live out are absorbed by those who watch us, carried on by those we influence, and repeated in ways we may never see. The shoebox reminds us that legacy is built in the present tense, not only remembered in the past.

Each day carries the opportunity to build a legacy of lessons. Every conversation, every response to difficulty, every quiet act of kindness is part of the history we are writing without realizing it. You may not know you are teaching, but your patience in adversity is seen. You may not realize you are guiding, but your consistency and endurance inspire. You may not recognize you are leaving something lasting, but your focus, your loyalty, your ability to seek guidance all become examples to others. These are the legacies that ripple outward, shaping more lives than you can imagine.

You never know you are making history when you are living it. My father did not. He was doing his duty, writing letters, solving problems, and standing by his convictions. Yet in those daily choices, he built a life that continues to speak. And so it is with us. Every decision is a chance to live with intention. Every day is a page in the story of who we are becoming and what we will leave behind.

The question is not whether you will leave a legacy—you will. The question is what legacy you are shaping. Will it be one of patience, that steadies those who come after you? Will it be one of endurance, teaching perseverance through hardship? Will it be one of focus, showing how to turn problems into progress? Will it be one of allegiance, modeling faithfulness and integrity? Will it be one of guidance, offering direction through the wisdom you have received?

The lessons you live today will become tomorrow's inheritance. They will be told and retold, not always through written letters, but through the memories of those you touch. Legacy is not only what you do for yourself but what continues in others. Live each day with that awareness. Seek solutions when problems arise. Practice focus when distractions press in. Show patience when asked to wait. Endure when the path is long. Be loyal to your word and your values. And stay open to guidance, always willing to learn and to teach.

A shoebox of letters preserved a father's voice for his children and grandchildren. What will preserve yours? It might be stories, journals, lessons passed at the dinner table, or the memory of a consistent life lived with integrity. Whatever form it takes, know that every day you are building it. Legacy is not a single moment—it is the accumulation of many small moments lived with intention.

So live today with that awareness. Live as though each action matters, because it does. Live knowing that history is being written, not someday, but now. And in doing so, you will leave behind words and a legacy of lessons—an inheritance of character and love that will endure through generations.

ABOUT THE AUTHOR

Nancy Moorhouse is a writer, and former safe production leader in the heavy highway and aggregate industry. Her other books, available for purchase from Amazon include:

> *Scoop, Crush & Rocks: Life Lessons from the Gravel Pit*

> *Solution-Focused Living: Trust the Process Through Affirmations*

Nancy's other writings can be found in the 2014 and 2023 *Celebrating 365 Days of Gratitude* books. Her industry focused publications can be found on the Insurance Thought Leadership website.

She is currently working on her next book.